Summary

of

Turtles All the Way Down

John Green

Conversation Starters

By BookHabits

Tips for Using BookHabits Conversation Starters:

EVERY GOOD BOOK CONTAINS A WORLD FAR DEEPER THAN the surface of its pages. The characters and their world come alive through the words on the pages, yet the characters and its world still live on. Questions herein are designed to bring us beneath the surface of the page and invite us into the world that lives on. These questions can be used to:

- Foster a deeper understanding of the book
- Promote an atmosphere of discussion for groups
- Assist in the study of the book, either individually or corporately
- Explore unseen realms of the book as never seen before

About Us:

THROUGH YEARS OF EXPERIENCE AND FIELD EXPERTISE, from newspaper featured book clubs to local library chapters, *BookHabits* can bring your book discussion to life. Host your book party as we discuss some of today's most widely read books.

Table of Contents

Introducing *Turtles All the Way Down*

TURTLES ALL THE WAY DOWN, IS A YOUNG ADULT NOVEL BY JOHN GREEN which tackles mental illness, particularly obsessive-compulsive disorder as suffered by the main character. It also tells the story of two friends who go through episodes that strengthen as well as test their friendship, and young love complicated by mental instability and family drama.

Aza Holmes, 16, has an irrational fear of microbes. She has a callous on her finger that she constantly opens and disinfects to prevent microbes from taking over. She learns from her friend Daisy that billionaire Russell Pickett is wanted for committing fraud and had gone missing. There is a $100,000 reward for anybody who could give important information about his whereabouts. Aza and Daisy want the reward for themselves and decide to search for Pickett. They sneak into the Pickett residential compound and are caught by security. They are then confronted by Pickett's son Davis. Aza and Davis begin to like each other afterwards but Aza's anxiety disorder prevents her from fully enjoying the relationship. She also quarrels with Daisy when Aza learns that Daisy had been complaining about Aza's obsessive character in her blog. Aza figures in a car accident after her fight with her friend and ends being hospitalized for weeks. The two girls resume their friendship after making amends. The mystery of the missing billionaire is soon to be solved as the two girls went exploring in a tunnel and discover a bad smell. They think Pickett's body is in there because it is part of the Pickett construction project. They tell Davis about it and he makes an anonymous call to the police who eventually discover Pickett's body in the tunnel. Davis knows that his father willed all his wealth to his pet tuatara, causing Davis and his brother to leave for Colorado. Aza and Davis part ways and Aza ponders her future.

The novel is told from the first-person perspective of Aza. Her obsessive character is revealed through her inner dialogue which is myopic and self-centered. The novel has the elements typical of young adult novels namely the central character of a troubled young narrator, misunderstanding between teens and adults, a love interest, even a scene where boy and girl look at the stars together, and a weird best friend. The tone and dialogue often become sentimental. The troubled teen characters are adeptly portrayed by the author. Aza, though anxious and obsessive, is also clear about her mental ailment. She thinks she does not have a choice where her anxiety disorder is concerned. Davis is a privileged boy who lives in a mansion, is sad about his mother's absence in his life, and now faces the unexplained disappearance of his father. He knows that if his father died, his fortune will all go to a pet reptile. Daisy is overbearing but has an endearing side to her. The novel paints a teenage world filled with Star Wars fan fiction, crushes, dates, and texting. The characters are articulate and self-aware. They express themselves and converse with each other with much wit. Critics describe the novel as funny and clever. It has the elements of a mystery thriller as the plot shows two friends trying to solve riddle of the missing billionaire, with a murky river and a mysterious mansion for setting. The main themes of the book, however is not the mystery but the mental illness that grips Aza, and the friendship and love among the teen characters. The novel adeptly touches on teen predicaments and issues like coming of age and pressures on the youth. The novel poses questions about what happy endings are all about, and how love can be understood as a tragedy or defeat. The author's expert handling of his theme brings readers to a heartfelt understanding of mental illness through the difficulties experienced by the main character. The theme of learning to accept one's inner demons and imperfections is also explored. Pop culture is a strong presence in the novel as referred to by the characters who dish out raves and criticisms about Iron Man, James Joyce, *The Tempest*, and *Jupiter Ascending*.

Written by the author of the #1 New York Times bestseller *The Fault in Our Stars, Turtles All The Way Down* was well-received by critics when it was released in October 2017. *The New York Times* praised it, calling it "surprising and moving." Other critics called it authentic and truthful. *The Guardian* said it could turn out to be "a new modern classic."

Discussion Questions

"Get Ready to Enter a New World"

Tip: Begin with questions dealing with broader issues to ensure ample time for quality discussions. Read through all discussion questions before engaging.

~~~

question 1

Turtles All the Way Down tells the story of two friends who go through episodes that strengthen as well as test their friendship, and young love complicated by mental instability and family drama. What makes this novel different from other young adult novels? Does it tackle a unique theme?

~~~

~~~

question 2

The novel tackles mental illness, particularly obsessive-compulsive disorder, as suffered by the main character, Aza. How is OCD described in the novel? Do know somebody close to you who has this disorder?

~~~

question 3

Aza has a callous on her finger that she constantly opens and disinfects to prevent microbes from taking over. How do you feel about the obsession about her finger? Can you understand why she has to keep opening and cleaning it?

~~~

question 4

Aza and Daisy decide to search for Pickett so they can have the $100,000 reward offered to whoever could provide information to about Pickett. They sneak into the Pickett residential compound and are caught by security. What can you say about Aza and Daisy having decided to look for Pickett? What kind of girls are they based on this?

~~~

question 5

Aza and Davis end up liking each other but Aza's mental disorder prevents her from fully enjoying the relationship. What is she anxious about when she is with Davis? Does she like being with Davis?

~~~

question 6

Aza quarrels with Daisy when she learns that Daisy had been complaining about Aza's obsessive character in her blog. Aza figures in a car accident after her fight with her friend and ends being hospitalized for weeks. The two girls resume their friendship after making amends. What kind of friendship do the two girls have? How do you feel about them reconciling?

~~~

question 7

Aza and Daisy tell Davis that his father is probably in the tunnel where they earlier explored. The police soon confirm that the body decomposing in the tunnel is Pickett. How do you feel about Davis who had to tip the police about his father's dead body in the tunnel? Do you think it was wise of the two girls to tell Davis first instead of the police?

~ ~ ~

~ ~ ~

question 8

Aza and Davis part ways after he after his father's death. How do you feel about the separation? Do you like the way the novel ends?

~ ~ ~

question 9

The novel is told from the first-person perspective of Aza. How does Aza's perspective affect the way the story is told? How does it make you feel as a reader?

question 10

The novel's tone and dialogue often become sentimental. How do you feel about the sentimentality? Do you think this is appropriate for a young adult novel?

question 11

Davis is the son of a wealthy man. He is sad about his mother's absence in his life, and now faces the unexplained disappearance of his father. How does he face these difficulties and sad circumstances in his life?

~~~

question 12

Daisy is overbearing but has an endearing side to her. Is there anything in her that you like? Why do you think she is overbearing?

~~~

question 13

Davis' father willed his fortune to a pet tuatara. Why do you think he does this? What kind of person is he?

~ ~ ~

~~~

question 14

The novel has the elements of a mystery thriller as the plot shows two friends looking for a missing man, with a murky river and a mysterious mansion for setting. Do you think the author intended this to be a mystery thriller? Why? Why not?

~~~

question 15

The theme of learning to accept one's inner demons and imperfections is explored in the novel. Can you cite particular instances where this is shown?

~~~

question 16

The New York Times review says the novel is "wrenching and revelatory." Can you cite parts of the novel that is wrenching? Why do you think the review called it revelatory?

~~~

~~~

question 17

People review says the novel is about "learning to cope when the world feels out of control." How do Ava and Davis cope with their difficult situations? Do they cope well?

~~~

question 18

The novel is "deeply honest" according to *Mashable*. What was it honest about? Do you like the author's honesty? Do you learn anything from the honesty?

~~~

question 19

School Library Journal review says the novel "informs and enlightens readers even as it breaks their hearts." Do you think it is a good combination in a novel to inform, enlighten and break readers' hearts at the same time? Why? Why not?

~~~

question 20

Green is a master of teen conversation according to *The Guardian*. Do you agree with the review? Which particular conversation in the novel captured your interest? Why?

Introducing the Author

AFTER HIS BESTSELLING *THE FAULT IN OUR STARS* came out in 2012, John Green attempted to write a new novel but anxiety attacks and fearfulness prevented him. His bestseller caused him to worry about having to replicate the book's success. He started new novels but abandoned them eventually. His mind was crowded with obsessive thoughts and he felt like these were imposed on him from the outside. He worried, for example, that he will not be able to write another book. Fortunately, he was able to come out of it in 2015 through medication coupled with therapy. He started writing about the experience and that is how *Turtles All The Way Down* came about. Green admits that he has had obsessive compulsive disorder (OCD) since he was a child. This latest book of his is the most personal and emotionally charged. His brother Hank says that it was only when he first read John's finished novel was he able to understand how it felt like to live with the mental illness. He never understood his brother's struggle with OCD until he read his work. In the book, Green acknowledges his doctors and his family for being supportive. He says he wanted to talk about the illness and not be embarrassed or be ashamed of it. He hopes the book will help others understand what people suffering with OCD go through. He also wants to show those afflicted with it that they can still live fulfilling lives provided they manage it well with the help of their families.

Green has written seven books so far, and has 50 million of these printed and distributed worldwide. He is known for his young adult novels whose characters have endeared themselves to readers for being witty and sensitive. His books' themes include illness and death, bullying, depression, and mental issues.

His first novel is the semiautobiographical *Looking for Alaska*, released in 2005. It is a story about a student living in a boarding house who is often bullied. The novel became a *New York Times* bestseller for children's paperback in 2012. *An Abundance of Katherines* is Green's second novel. It is a Printz Award runner-up and a Los Angeles Times Book Prize finalist. This was followed by other young adult novels *Paper Towns*, and *Will Grayson* which he co-authored with David Levithan. *Paper Towns* was adapted into film and released in July 2015. *The Fault in Our Stars* became an international bestseller with 23 million printed copies and was adapted into film. This number one box-office hit features the bittersweet story of two young lovers afflicted with cancer. *Turtles* will also be adapted into film soon, according to Green.

Green is also known for his YouTube channel known as VlogBrothers. Other online events which he launched with his brother include Project for Awesome and Vicon. His educational online show called Crash Course teaches courses like literature, science, history, economics, US government, astronomy, among others. The shows have attracted over two billion views. The author is cited by *Time* magazine as among the 100 Most Influential People in the World in 2014.

He lives in Indianapolis with wife Sarah Urist and children Henry and Alice, aged 7 and 4 respectively.

Fireside Questions

"What would you do?"

Tip: These questions can be a fun exercise as it spurs creativity among the readers by allowing alternate scene endings and "if this was you" questions.

question 21

John Green suffered obsessive-compulsive disorder (OCD) since he was a child. His latest book reveals how it feels like to have OCD. Why did he write about his ailment in his novel? How will it affect people who are also afflicted with OCD?

question 22

His brother Hank says that it was only when he first read John's finished novel was he able to understand how it felt like to live with the mental illness. He never understood his brother's struggle with OCD until he read his work. How does the book enlighten you about OCD? Does it change your perception of the disease?

question 23

He is known for his young adult novels whose characters have endeared themselves to readers for being witty and sensitive. Which characters in the book reflect wit and sensitivity? Can you cite instances where they particularly displayed these characteristics?

~~~

~~~

question 24

His novel *The Fault in Our Stars* became an international bestseller with 23 million printed copies and was adapted into film. This number one box-office hit features the bittersweet story of two young lovers afflicted with cancer. Why do you think the book became a bestseller? Have you read the book? Why do you like or dislike it?

~~~

~~~

question 25

Time magazine cited Green as among the 100 Most Influential People in the World in 2014. What about his books make him influential? Why are his themes relevant to many?

~~~

~~~

question 26

Aza the protagonist has an obsessive character revealed through her inner dialogue which is myopic and self-centered. If Aza is a boy, how different would the story be? Do you think the friendship with Daisy would totally change? How?

~~~

question 27

Davis' father willed his fortune to his pet tuatara. If the wealth goes to Davis instead, how will it change Davis' character? Will you like the story better if this is the case?

~~~

question 28

Aza has obsessive-compulsive disorder. If she suffers depression instead, how will her inner dialogue change? Would she still be friends with Daisy? How will her relationship with Davis change?

~~~

~~~

question 29

The novel is told from the first-person perspective of Aza. If the story is told from a third person perspective, what will the effect be on the tone of the story? Would you prefer Aza's voice to that of a third person's voice?

~~~

question 30

Aza and Daisy are best friends. If the friendship turns into something romantic, how will it affect the story? Would it be more interesting?

Quiz Questions

"Ready to Announce the Winners?"

Tip: Create a leaderboard and track scores to see who gets the most correct answers. Winners required. Prizes optional.

quiz question 1

The novel explores _____ as a mental disorder. Aza is afflicted with it.

quiz question 2

The billionaire _____ is wanted for committing fraud and had gone missing. There is a $100,000 reward for anybody who could give important information about his whereabouts.

quiz question 3

_____ knows that if his father died, his fortune will all go to a pet reptile.

quiz question 4

True or False: The novel has the elements of a mystery thriller. The plot shows two friends trying to solve riddle of the missing billionaire, with a murky river and a mysterious mansion for setting.

~~~

quiz question 5

True or False: The main theme of the book is the mystery of the missing billionaire.

~~~

~~~

quiz question 6

True or False: The author's expert handling of his theme brings readers to a heartfelt understanding of mental illness through the difficulties experienced by the main character.

~~~

quiz question 7

True or False: The theme of learning to accept one's inner demons and imperfections is also explored.

~ ~ ~

quiz question 8

Green is known for his _____ novels peopled
with teen characters and their issues of bullying,
illness and death, and depression.

~ ~ ~

quiz question 9

His novel _____ became an international bestseller with 23 million printed copies and was adapted into film. This number one box-office hit features the bittersweet story of two young lovers afflicted with cancer.

~~~

quiz question 10

True or False: Green has a YouTube channel known as VlogBrothers which he set up with his brother Hank.

~~~

quiz question 11

True or False: He is cited by *The New York Times* as among the 100 Most Influential People in the World in 2014.

~~~

quiz question 12

True or False: Like *The Fault in Our Stars, Turtles All the Way Down* will also be adapted into film soon.

~~~

Quiz Answers

1.   obsessive-compulsive disorder
2.   Russell Pickett
3.   Davis
4.   True
5.   False
6.   True
7.   True
8.   young adult
9.   The Fault in Our Stars
10.   True
11.   False
12.   True

Ways to Continue Your Reading

E VERY month, our team runs through a wide selection of books to pick the best titles for readers and reading groups, and promotes these titles to our thousands of readers – sometimes with free downloads, sale dates, and additional brochures.

If you have not yet read the original work or would like to read it again, get the book here.

Want to register yourself or a book group? It's free and takes 1-click.

Register here.

On the Next Page…

Please write us your reviews! Any length would be fine but we'd appreciate hearing you more! We'd be SO grateful.

Till next time,

BookHabits

"Loving Books is Actually a Habit"

Lightning Source UK Ltd.
Milton Keynes UK
UKHW011000101019
351356UK00001B/202/P